PRAISE

Arranged for Easy Piano by Carol Tornquist

Now you can play the music from church that you love to hear and sing with the *Pure & Simple* series. Each book features lyrics, suggested fingerings, phrasing, pedal markings, and easy-to-read notation. The solo piano arrangements, which use familiar harmonies and rhythms, will put your favorite melodies at your fingertips quickly and easily.

This volume features praise songs, which are an important part of contemporary worship services. Praise music's large and loyal following enjoys the simple and memorable melodies and the folk, pop, and rock rhythms. The uplifting lyrics make praise music perfect for personal moments of reflection as well as sing-along gatherings with loved ones. Additionally, praise music is a valuable addition to any pianist's repertoire of traditional worship songs.

Produced by
Alfred Music Publishing Co., Inc.
P.O. Box 10003
Van Nuys, CA 91410-0003
alfred.com

Printed in USA.

ISBN-10: 0-7390-5936-X
ISBN-13: 978-0-7390-5936-4

CONTENTS

Better Is One Day

Words and Music by Matt Redman
Arranged by Carol Tornquist

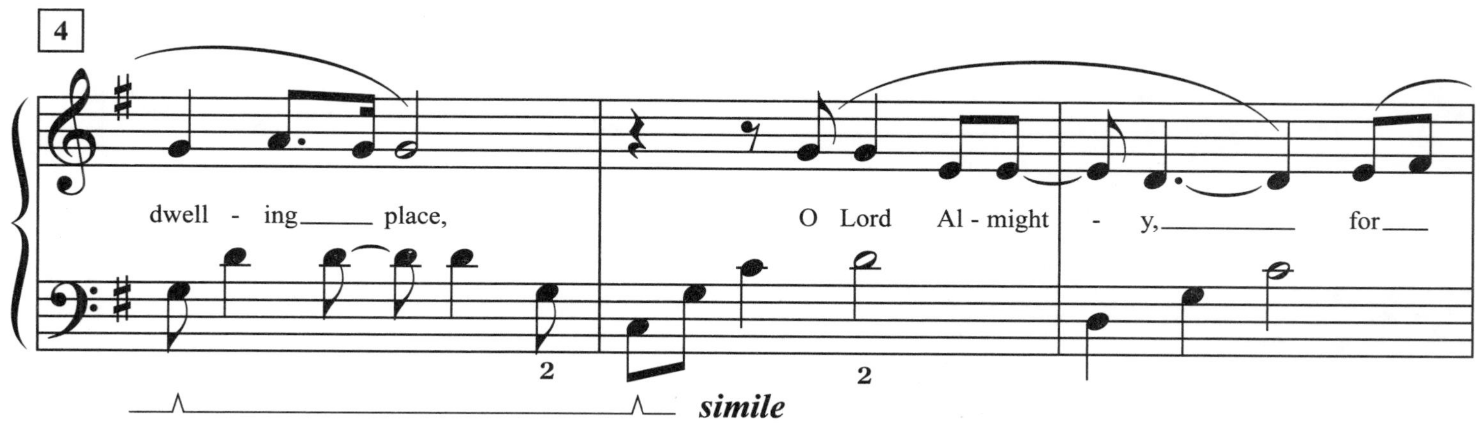

10
For here my heart is sat - is - fied
5
2

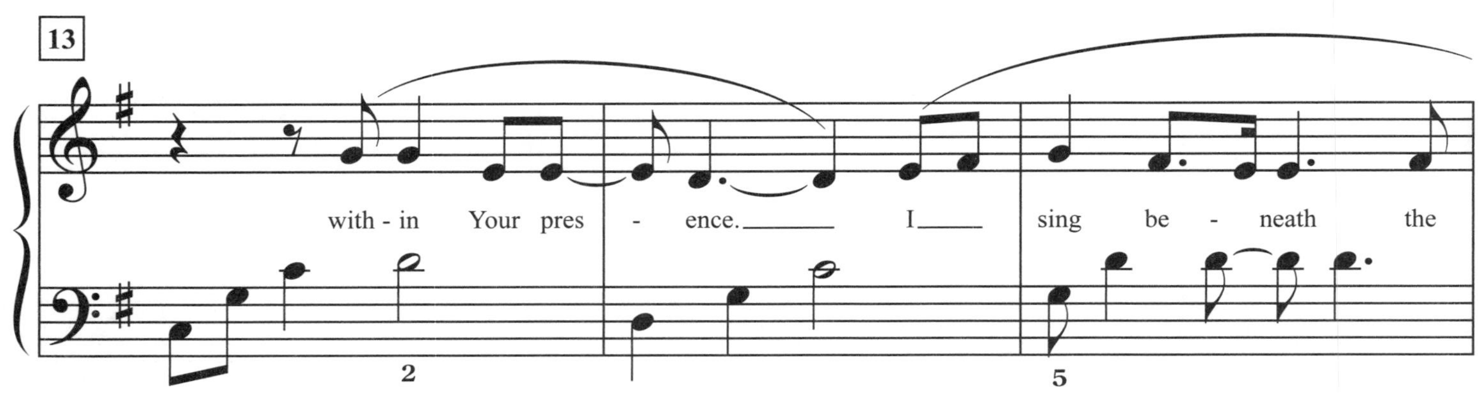
13
with - in Your pres - ence. I sing be - neath the
2
5

16
shad - ow of Your wings. Bet-ter is
2
mf

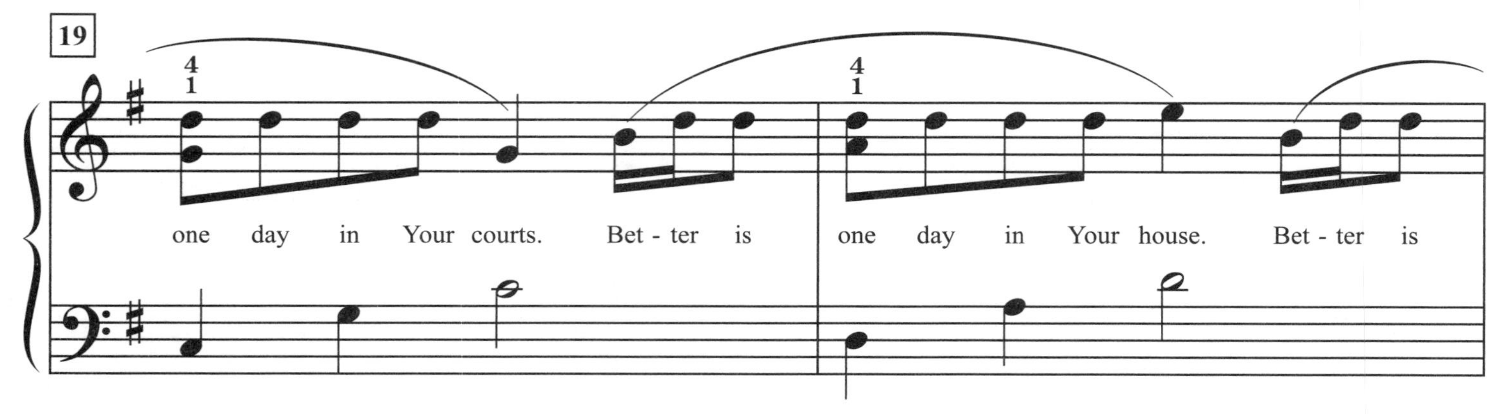
19
4
1
one day in Your courts. Bet - ter is one day in Your house. Bet - ter is

21
one day in Your courts than thou - sands
else - where.
Bet - ter is

23
one day in Your courts.
Bet - ter is
one day in Your house.
Bet - ter is

25
one day in Your courts than thou - sands
else - where,
than thou - sands

27
else - where.
One
thing I ask and
mp

30
I would seek:
to see Your beau - ty, to
33
find You in the place Your glo - ry dwells.
36
Bet - ter is one day in Your courts. Bet - ter is
mf
38
one day in Your house. Bet - ter is one day in Your courts than thou - sands

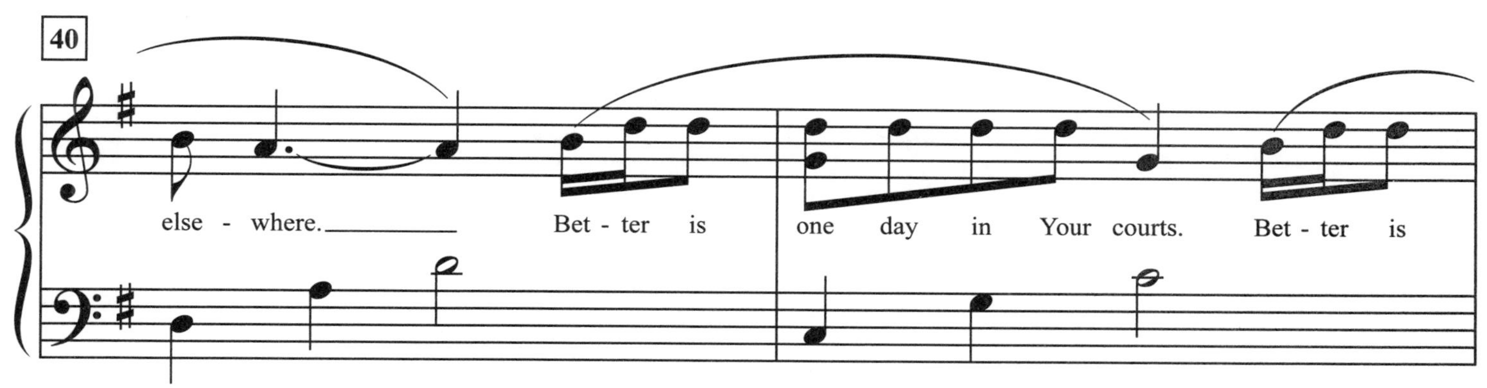
40
else - where.
Bet - ter is
one day in Your courts.
Bet - ter is

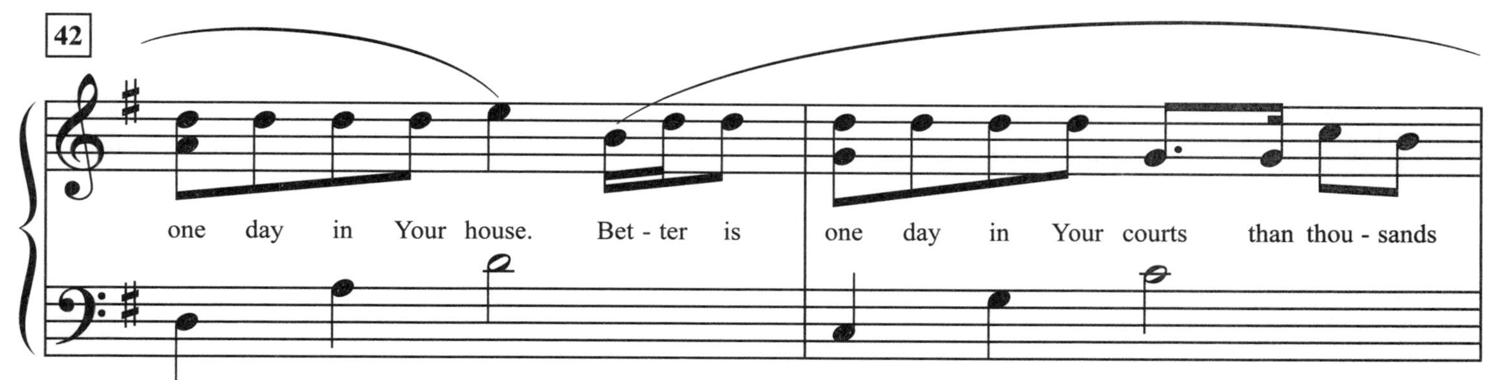
42
one day in Your house.
Bet - ter is
one day in Your courts
than thou - sands

44
2
else - where,
than thou - sands
else - where.
5

46
rit.
mp
4

Amazing Grace (My Chains Are Gone)

Words and Music by
Chris Tomlin and Louie Giglio
Arranged by Carol Tornquist

10
now am found; was blind, but now I see. My chains are
13
mf
gone, I've been set free. My God, my Sav - ior has ran-somed
16
me. And like a flood His mer - cy reigns, un - end - ing
19
love, a - maz - ing grace. The earth shall soon dis -
mp

22
solve like snow, the sun for - bear to shine. But
25
God, who called me here be - low, will be for - ev - er
28
mine. My chains are gone, I've been set
mf
30
free. My God, my Sav - ior has ran - somed

32
me.
And like a
flood
His mer - cy
34
reigns,
un - end - ing
love,
a - maz - ing
36
grace.
39
rit.

Blessed Be Your Name

Words and Music by
Beth Redman and Matt Redman
Arranged by Carol Tornquist

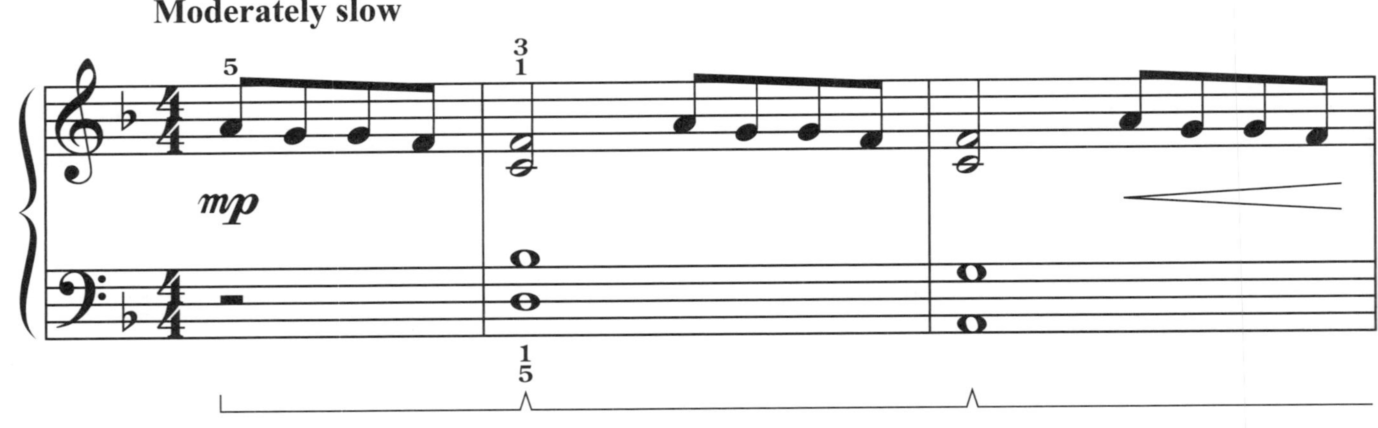

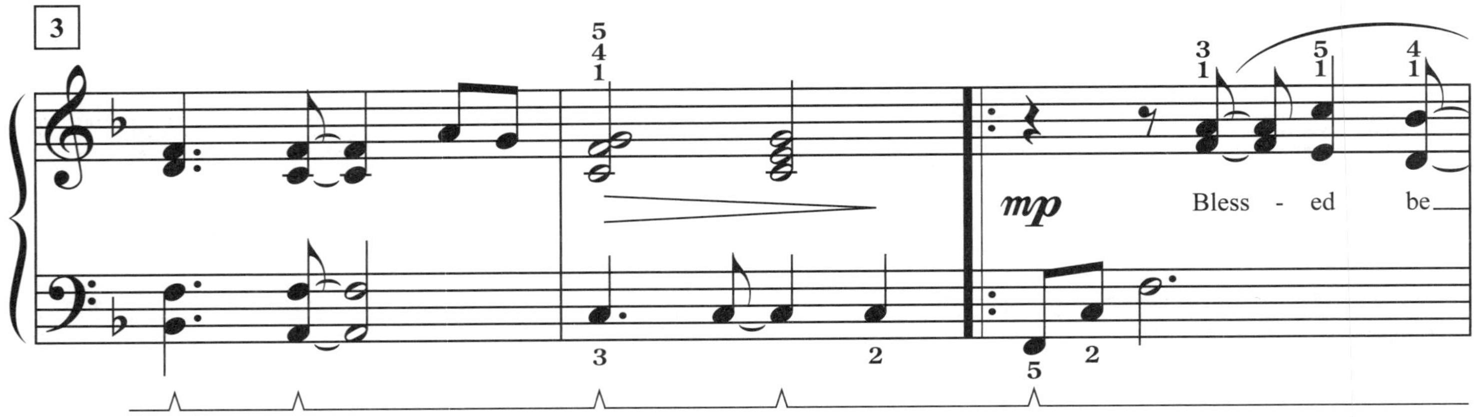

8
- ti - ful,
where Your
streams
of
a - bun -
10
- dance flow,
bless - ed
be Your name.
13
Bless - ed
be
Your
name
when I'm
15
found
in
the
des
- ert
place,
though I

17
walk through the wil - der - ness, blessed be Your name.
20
Ev-'ry bless-ing You pour out I'll turn back to
24
praise. When the dark-ness clos-es in, Lord, still I will
28
say: Bless-ed be the name of the Lord, bless-ed be Your
mf

31
name.
Bless - ed be the name of the Lord,
34
bless - ed be Your glo - ri - ous name!
dim.
37
1.
2.
mp
40
Slowly
rit.
p

BREATHE

Words and Music by Marie Barnett
Arranged by Carol Tornquist

10
- ence
liv - ing
in me.
13
This is my
dai - ly bread,
this is my
16
dai - ly bread;
Your ver - y Word
spo - ken
to me.
20
And
mp
I,
I'm des - p'rate for

23
You.
And I,
26
1.
I'm lost with-out You.
29
2.
p
This is the air I breathe,
32
this is the air I breathe.
rit.

Great Is the Lord

Words and Music by
Michael W. Smith and Deborah D. Smith
Arranged by Carol Tornquist

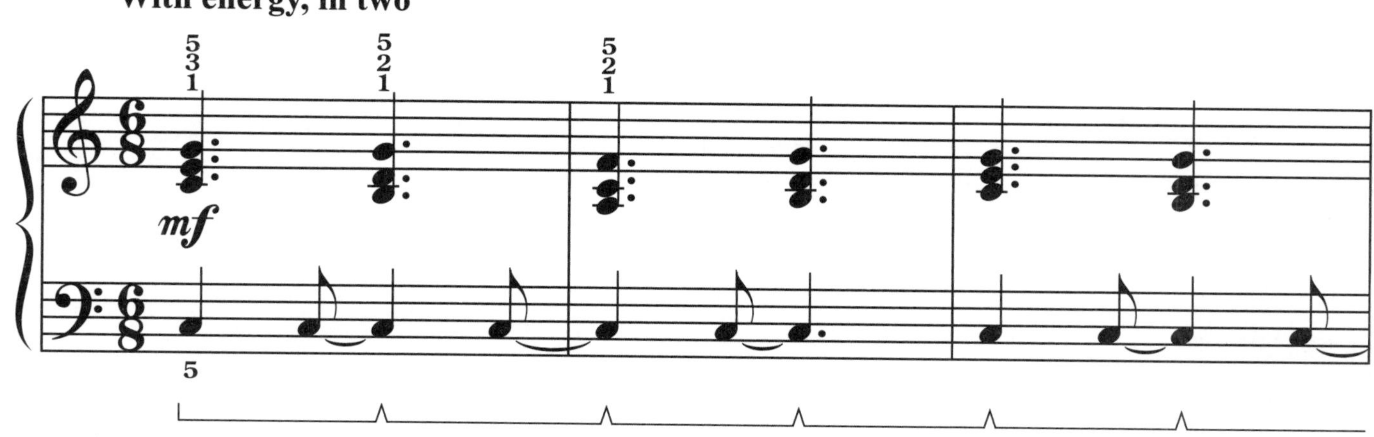

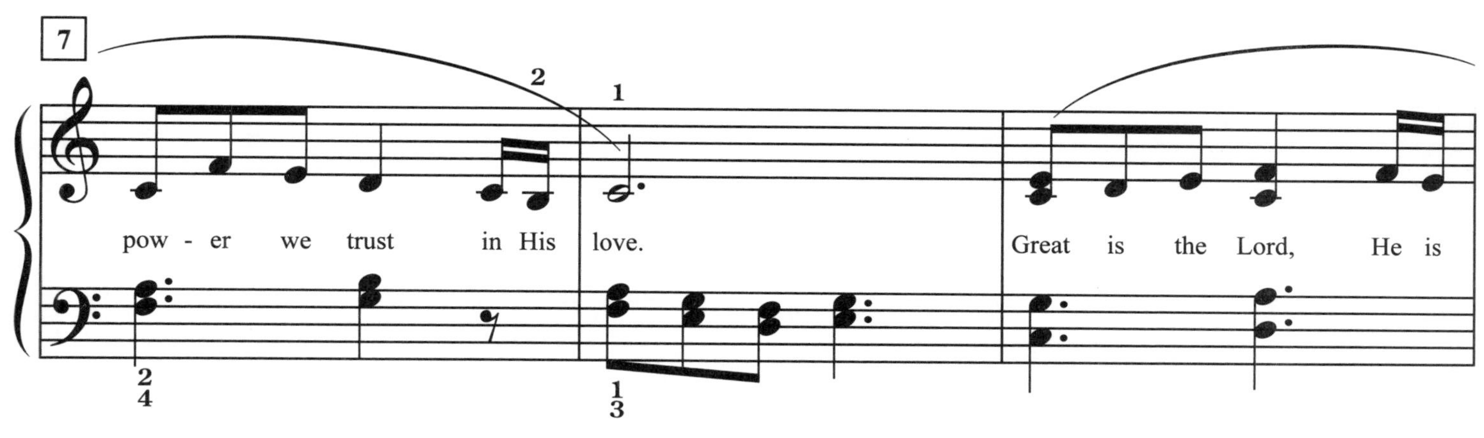

10
faith - ful and true; by His mer - cy He proves He is love.
13
Great is the Lord and wor - thy of glo - ry! Great is the Lord and
16
wor - thy of praise. Great is the Lord; now lift up your voice, now
cresc.
19
lift up your voice:
f
Great is the

Lord!
Great
is the
Lord!
dim.
Great is the Lord, He is
mf
ho - ly and just; by His
pow - er we trust in His
love.

34
Great is the Lord, He is faith - ful and true; by His mer - cy He proves He is

37
love.
Great are You, Lord, and wor - thy of glo - ry!

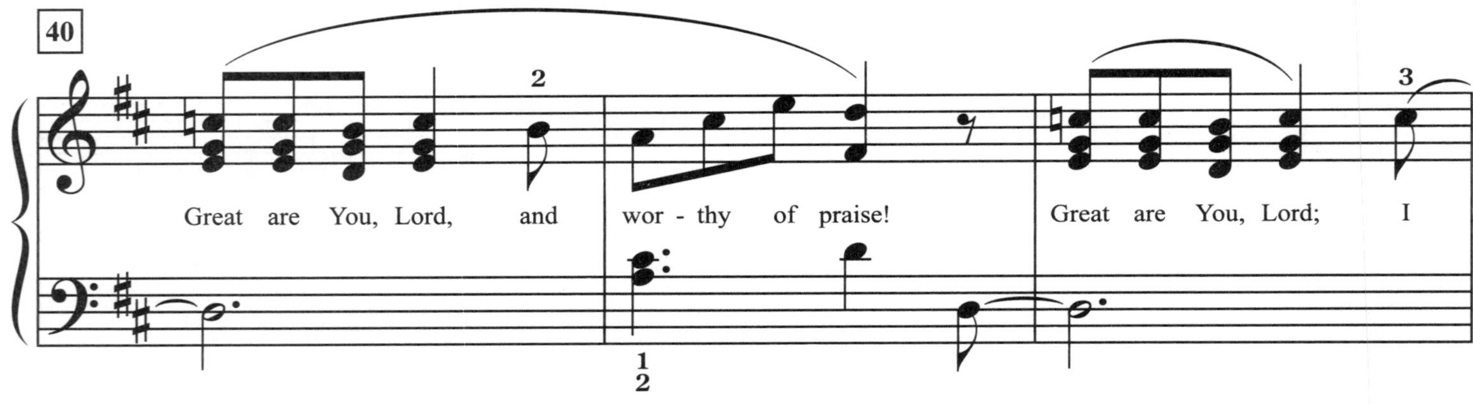
40
Great are You, Lord, and wor - thy of praise! Great are You, Lord; I

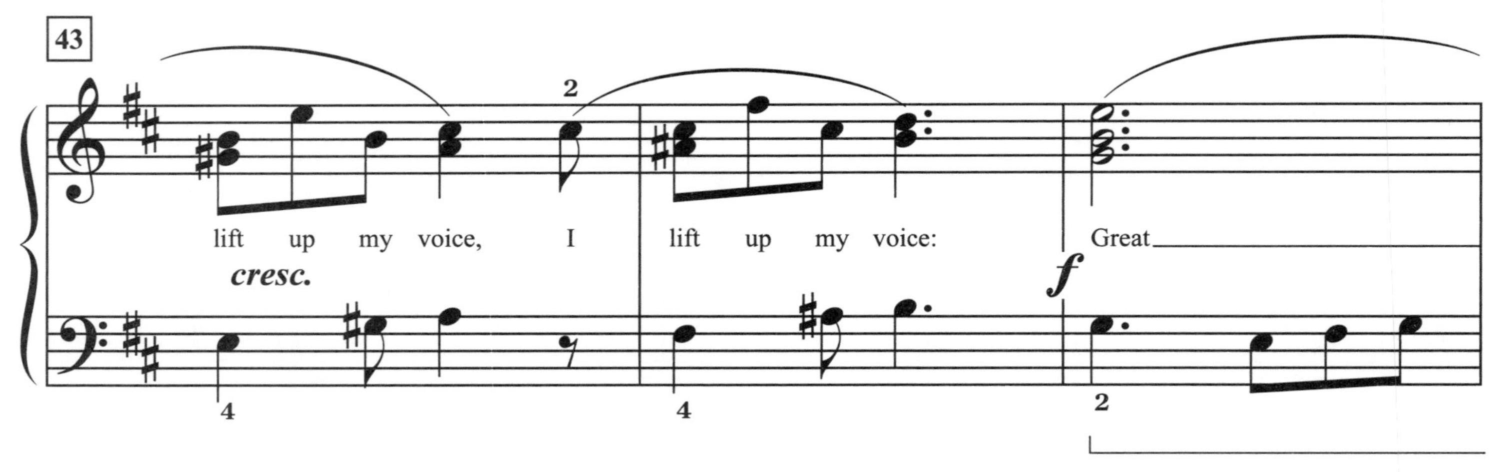
43
lift up my voice, I lift up my voice: Great
cresc.

46
are You,
Lord!
2
5
2
49
Great
are You,
Lord!
1
3
52
simile
55
ff

FOREVER

Words and Music by Chris Tomlin
Arranged by Carol Tornquist

Moderately, in two

10
God and King. His love en - dures for - ev - er.
out-stretched arm, His love en - dures for - ev - er.
13
For He is good, He is a - bove all things. His love en - dures for - ev -
For the life that's been re - born, His love en - dures for - ev -
16
- er.
- er.
Sing praise, sing
19
praise! Sing praise,

22
sing
praise!
For - ev -
mf
25
- er God is faith - ful,
for - ev
- er God is strong,
28
for - ev
- er God is with us,
for - ev -
31
- er.
1.
With a
mp
2.
for - ev -
mp

34
- er!
for - ev - er!
5

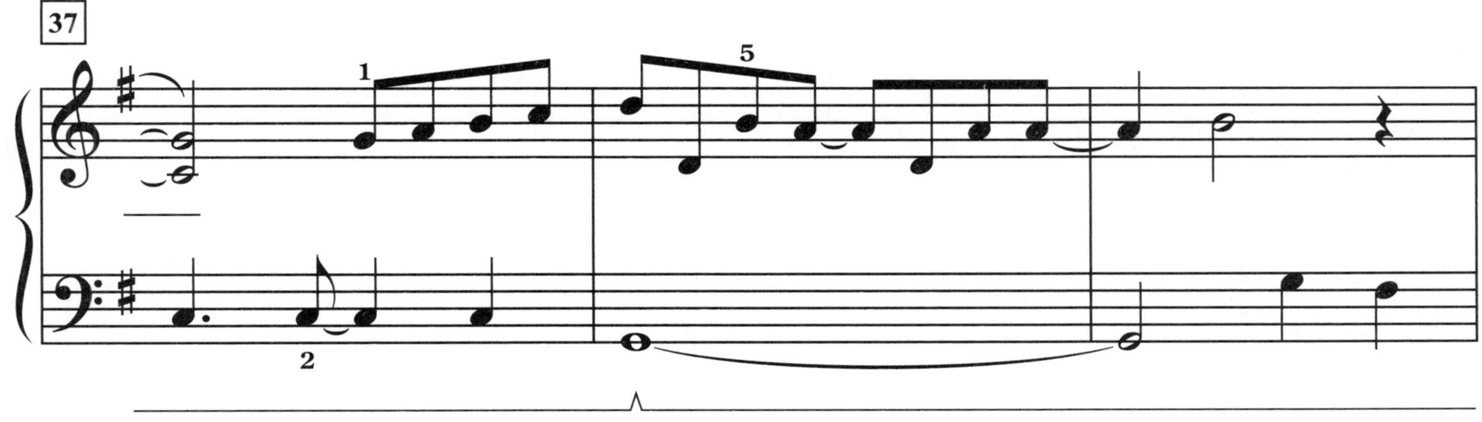
37
1
5
2

40
dim.
1

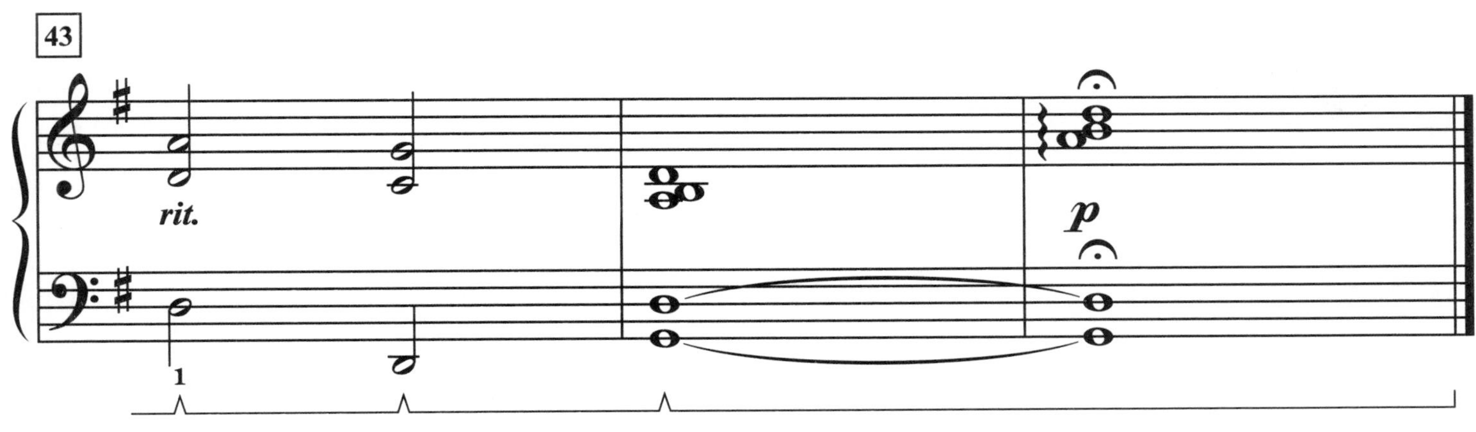
43
rit.
p
1

HALLELUJAH (YOUR LOVE IS AMAZING)

Words and Music by
Brenton Brown and Brian Doerksen
Arranged by Carol Tornquist

9
- ing, stead - y and un-chang - ing; Your love is a moun -
- ing. I can feel it ris - ing, all the joy that's grow -
5
11
2
3
- tain firm be-neath__ my feet. Your love is a mys -
- ing deep in-side__ of me. Ev - 'ry time I see__
5
13
- t'ry, how You gent - ly lift__ me; when I am sur-round -
__ You all Your good-ness shines__ through. I can feel this God__
15
2
5
1
- ed, Your love car - ries me.
__ song ris - ing up__ in me.
Hal - le - lu -
mf
5

17
- jah, hal - le - lu - jah, hal - le - lu -
19
- jah! Your love makes me sing. Hal - le - lu -
21
- jah, hal - le - lu - jah, hal - le - lu -
23
- jah! Your love makes me sing.

1.
2.
25
Your love is sur-pris-
mp
27
30
33
rit.
mp

He Knows My Name

Words and Music by Tommy Walker
Arranged by Carol Tornquist

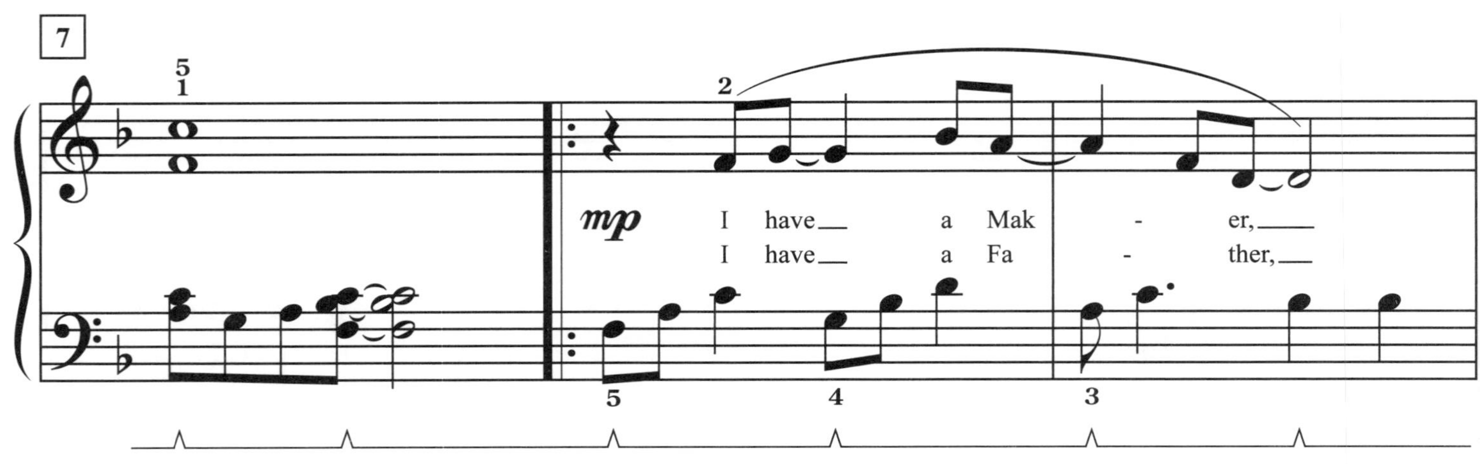

10
He formed my heart.
He calls me His own.
12
Be - fore e - ven time be - gan, my
He'll nev - er leave me, no
14
life was in His hands.
mat - ter where I go.
16
mf
He knows my name,
He knows my ev -

19
4
1
2
3
- 'ry thought.
He sees each tear that falls, and
1
5
22
1.
hears me when I
call.
dim.
2
4
25
2.
hears me when I
call.
He
hears me when I
1
2
1
28
call.
5
rit.
5
1
p

Holy Is the Lord

Words and Music by
Chris Tomlin and Louie Giglio
Arranged by Carol Tornquist

Moderately, with reverence

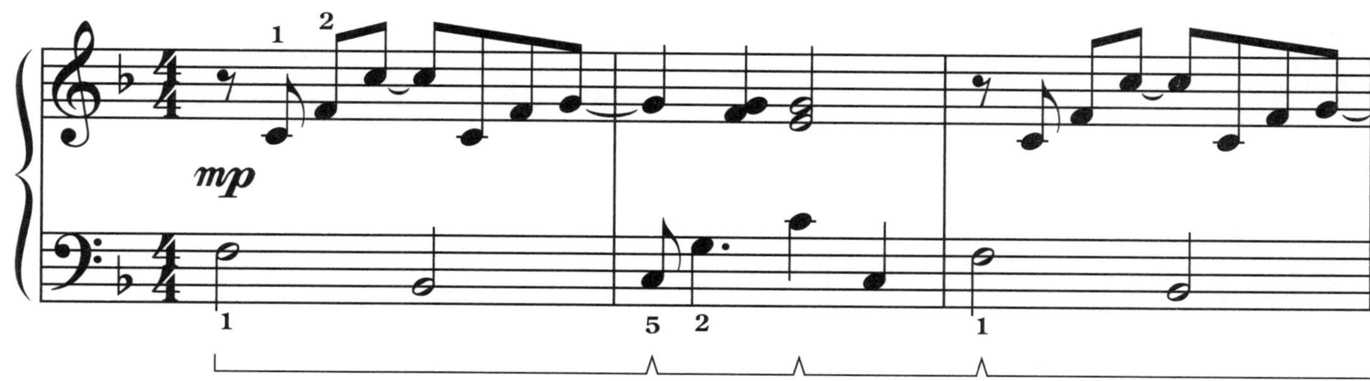

10
- ship Him now; how great, how awe - some is He! And to-geth-er we sing,
13
ev - 'ry - one sing:
16
mf
Ho - ly is the Lord God Al - might - y! The earth
19
is filled with His glo - ry. Ho - ly is the Lord God Al-might-

22
- y! The earth is filled with His glo - ry! The earth
25
is filled with His glo - ry! It is ris - ing up all
mp
3
5
28
a - round, it's the an - them of the Lord's re - nown. It's ris -
2
5
2
31
- ing up all a - round, it's the an - them of the Lord's
3
5

34
re - nown.
And to - geth - er we sing,
2
1
3
37
3
3
ev - 'ry - one
sing:
mf
3
Ho - ly is the
40
Lord God Al - might - y!
The earth is filled with His glo -
5
43
- ry! Ho - ly is the
Lord God Al - might - y!
The earth

46
is filled with His glo - ry! The earth is filled with His glo -
49
- ry! The earth is filled with His glo - ry!
52
Ho - ly, ho - ly is the Lord Al - might - y. Ho - ly, ho -
mp
55
1.
2.
ly.
ly.
rit.
p

How Great Is Our God

Words and Music by
Jesse Reeves, Chris Tomlin, and Ed Cash
Arranged by Carol Tornquist

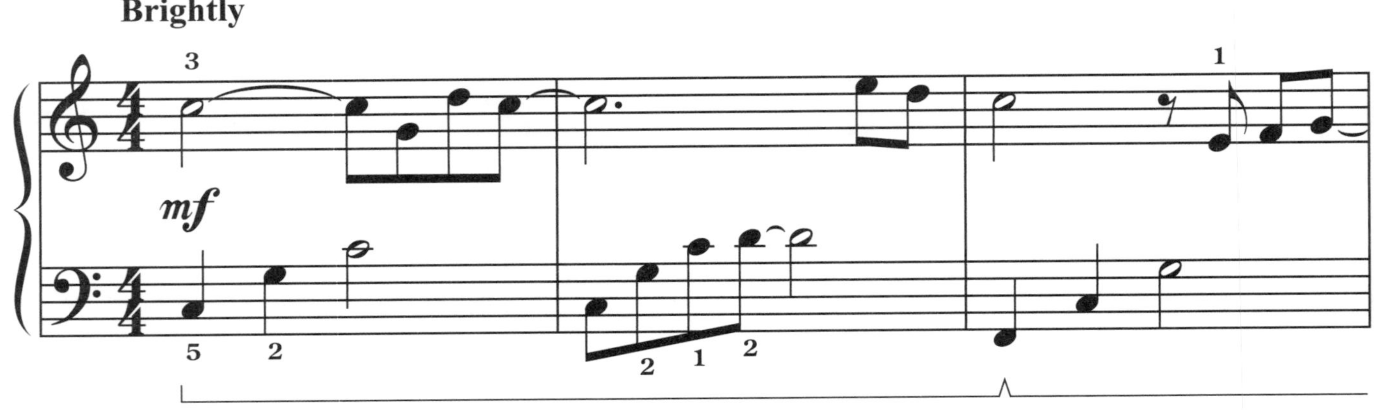

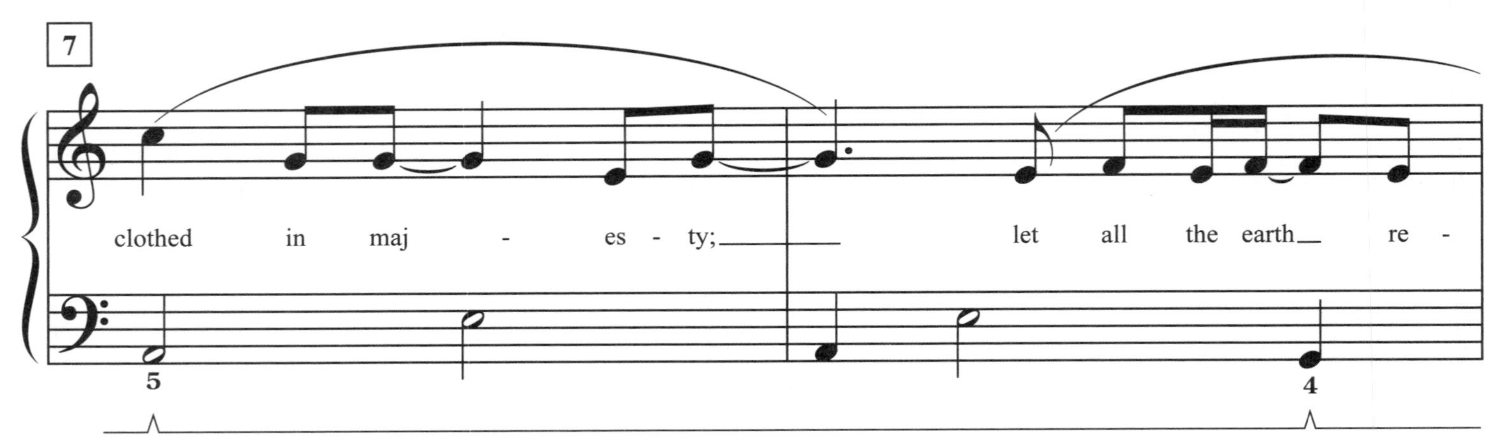

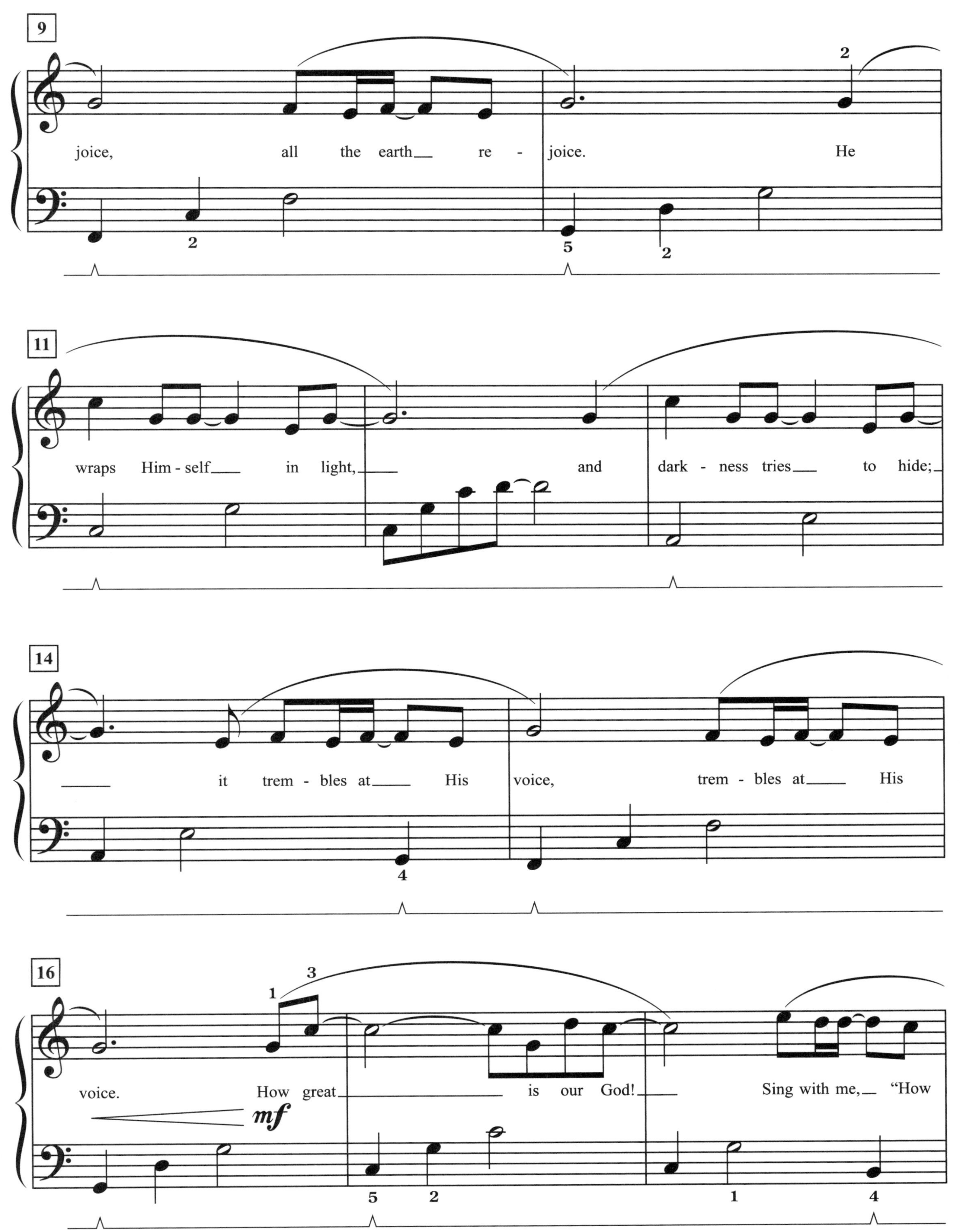
9
joice, all the earth re - joice. He
11
wraps Him - self in light, and dark - ness tries to hide;
14
it trem - bles at His voice, trem - bles at His
16
voice. How great is our God! Sing with me, "How
mf

19
great is our God!" And all will see how great, how great
22
is our God!
25
a tempo
rit.
Age to age He stands,
mp
28
and time is in His hands;

30
Be - gin - ning and the End, Be - gin - ning and the
5
4
32
2
End. The God - head, three in one,
mf
1
35
Fa - ther, Spir - it, Son, the Li - on and the
37
Lamb, the Li - on and the Lamb. How great
2
f
5

39
is our God!
Sing with me, "How
41
great is our God!"
And all will see how
great, how great
44
is our God!
47
rit.
mp

I Love You, Lord

Words and Music by Laurie Klein
Arranged by Carol Tornquist

10
You; oh, my soul, re - joice! Take joy, my King,
14
in what You hear; may it be a sweet, sweet
18
a tempo
sound in Your ear.
rit.
I
mf
21
praise You, Lord, and I lift my voice to

25
hon - or You; oh, my soul, re - joice! Take
29
joy, my King, in what You hear; may it be a
33
sweet, sweet sound in Your ear.
37
rit.
Very slowly
p

I Could Sing of Your Love Forever

Words and Music by Martin Smith
Arranged by Carol Tornquist

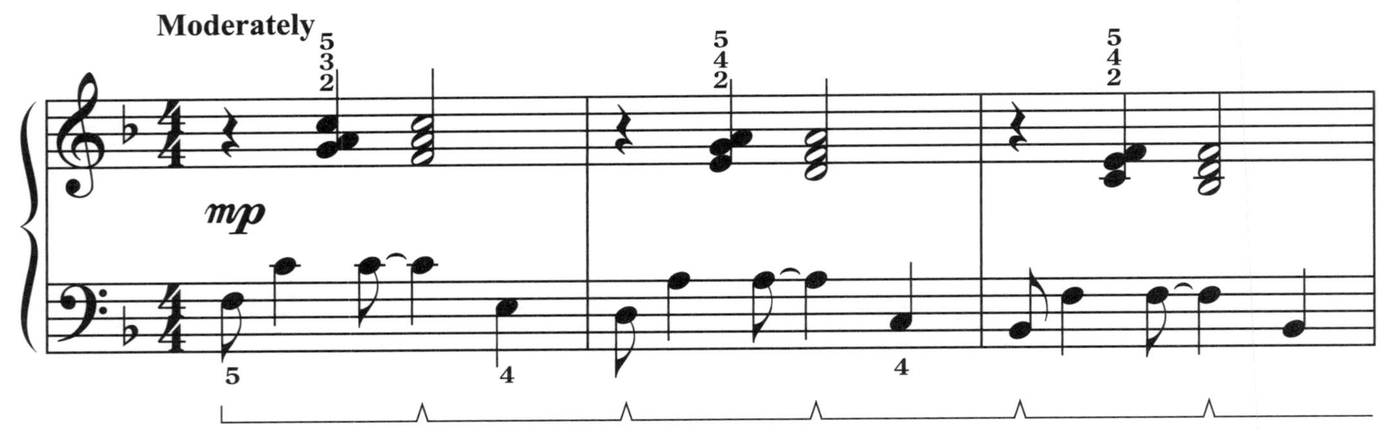

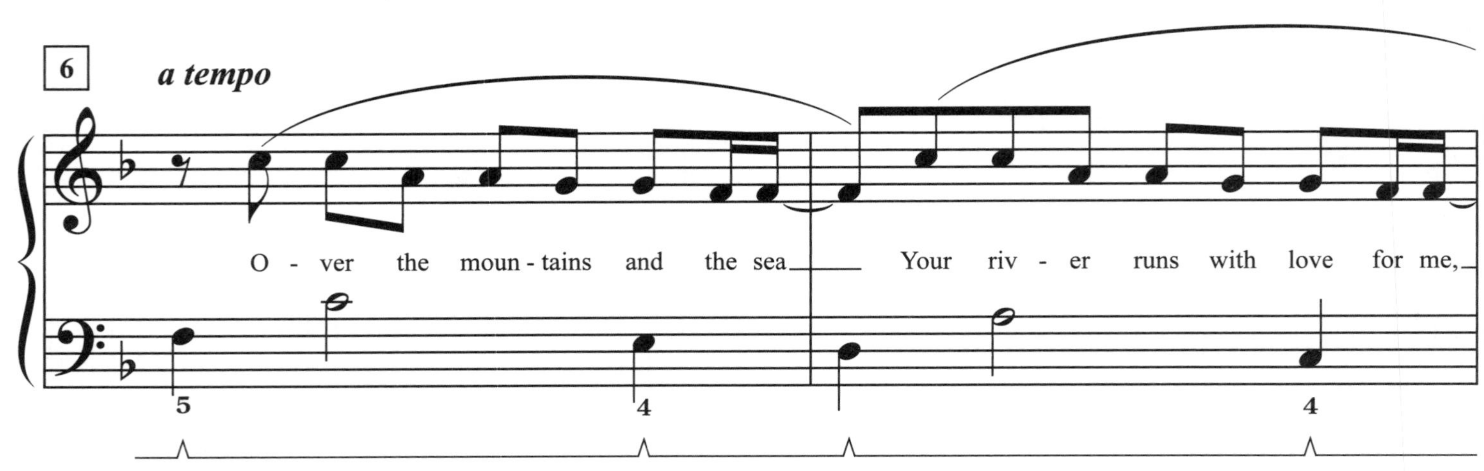

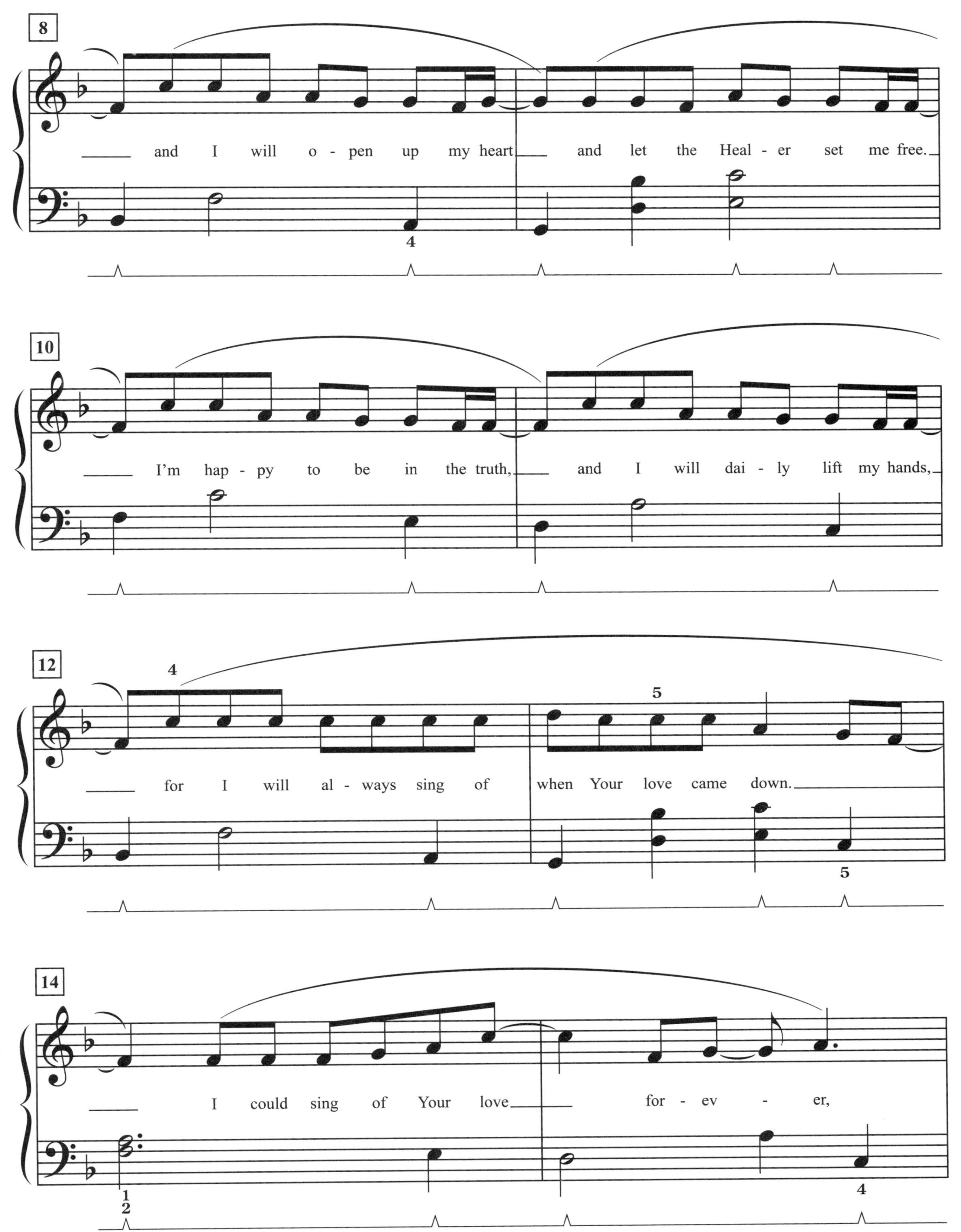
8
and I will o - pen up my heart
and let the Heal - er set me free.
4
10
I'm hap - py to be in the truth,
and I will dai - ly lift my hands,
12
4
for I will al - ways sing of
5
when Your love came down.
5
14
I could sing of Your love
for - ev - er,
1
2
4

16
I could sing of Your love
for - ev - er.
5
18
I could sing of Your love
for - ev - er,
20
I could sing of Your love
for - ev - er.
3
1
23
1
mf
I could sing of Your love
for - ev - er,

25
I could sing of Your love forev - er.
27
I could sing of Your love for - ev - er,
29
I could sing of Your love.
mp
5
4
32
2
1
1
rit.
p
4
3

In Christ Alone (My Hope Is Found)

Words and Music by
Stuart Townend and Keith Getty
Arranged by Carol Tornquist

9
stone, this sol - id
ground, firm through the
fierc - est drought and
12
storm. What heights of
love, what depths of
peace when fears are
15
stilled, when striv - ings
cease. My Com - fort -
er, my All in
18
All; here in the
love of Christ I
stand.

21
cresc.
24
No guilt in life, no fear in death; this is the
mf
27
power of Christ in me. From life's first cry to fi - nal
30
breath Je - sus com - mands my des - ti - ny. No power of

33
hell, no scheme of man can ev - er pluck me from His
f
dim.
36
hand. 'Til He re - turns or calls me
mf
38
home, here in the power of Christ I'll
rit.
40
Very slowly
stand!

IN THE SECRET (I WANT TO KNOW YOU)

Words and Music by Andy Park
Arranged by Carol Tornquist

10
in the qui - et
place,
for the high - est
goal
13
in the still - ness,
You are there.
that I might re - ceive the prize.
simile
16
In the se - cret,
in the qui - et
Press-ing on - ward,
push-ing ev - 'ry
2
19
ho - ur I wait
on - ly for You,
'cause I want to
hin-drance a - side,
out of my way,
'cause I want to
3
5
2
5

22
know You more.
know You more.
4
25
1
mf
I want to know You,
I want to hear Your voice;
29
I want to know You more.
2 1
33
I want to know You,
I want to see Your face;

37
1.
I want to know You more.
poco rit.
mp
5
2

41
2.
a tempo
mp

45

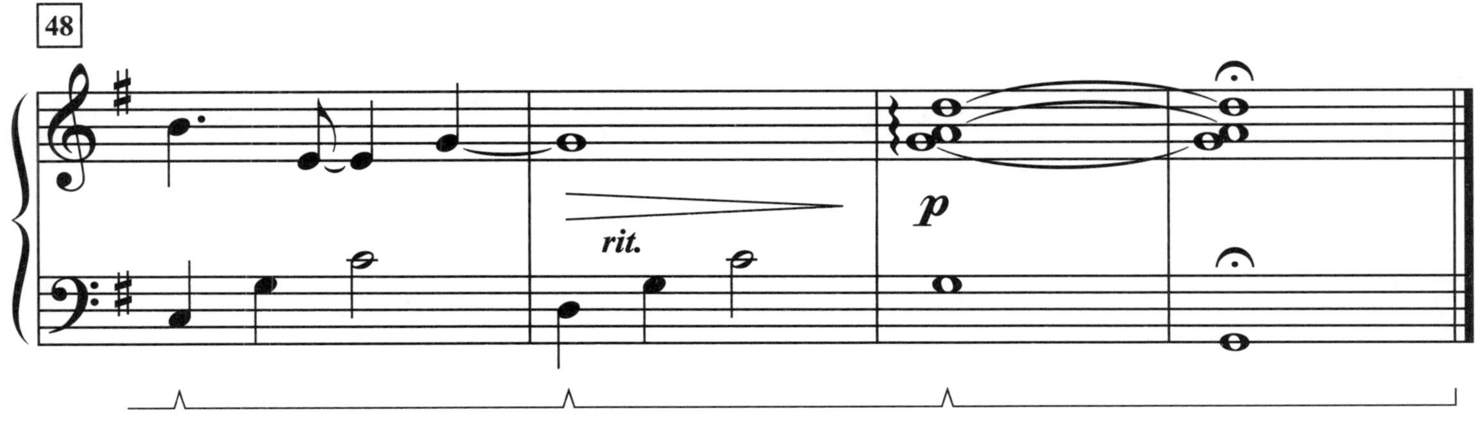
48
rit.
p

Sing to the King

Words and Music by Billy Foote
Arranged by Carol Tornquist

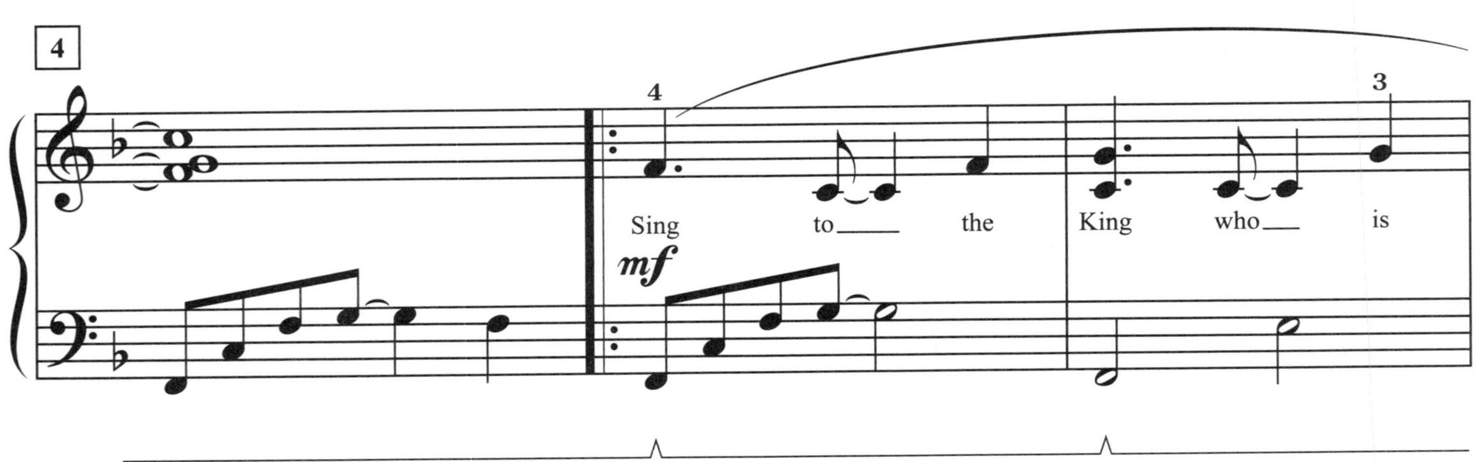

10
4
Je - sus, the Lamb that was slain.

13
3
Life and sal - va - tion His em - pire shall bring;

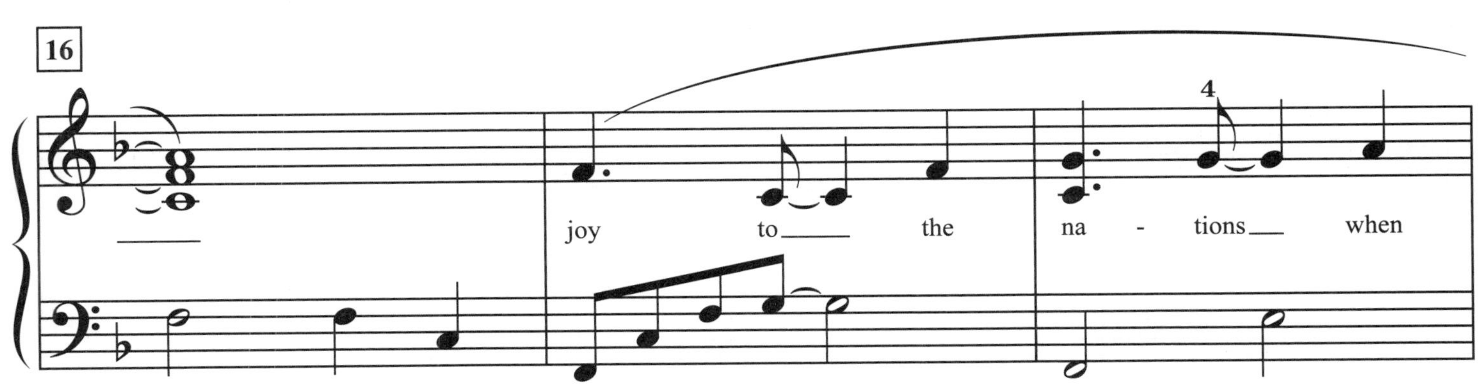
16
4
joy to the na - tions when

19
Je - sus is King.
22
Come, let us sing a song, a song de - clar - ing that we
25
be - long to Je - sus;
He is all we
28
need.
Lift up a heart

31
of praise;
sing now with voic - es raised to Je -
34
- sus.
Sing to the King.
37
1.
2.
Sing to the King.
40
Sing to the King.
rit.

Lord, I Lift Your Name on High

Words and Music by Rick Founds
Arranged by Carol Tornquist

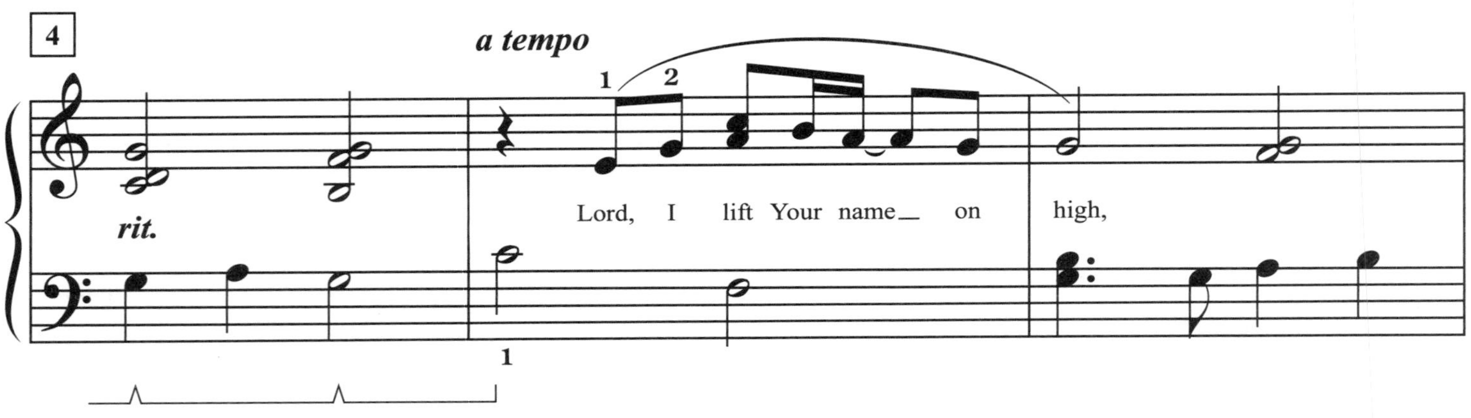

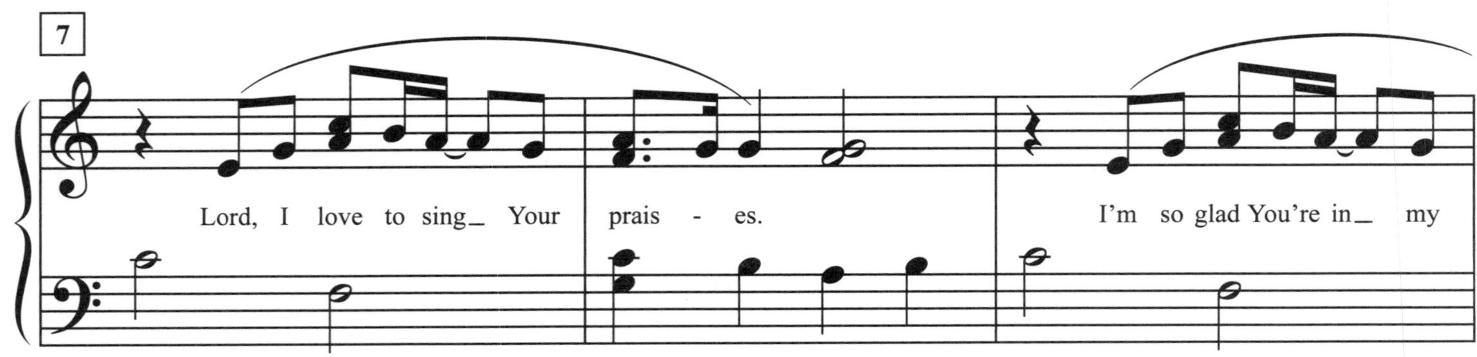

10
life.
I'm so glad You came to
save us.

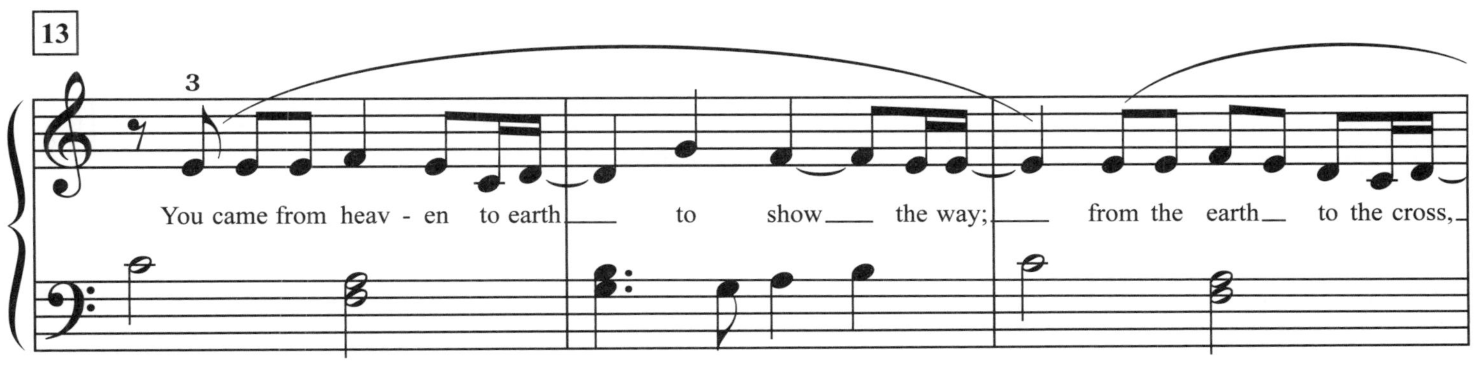
13
3
You came from heav - en to earth
to show the way;
from the earth to the cross,

16
my debt to pay.
From the cross to the grave,
4
from the grave to the sky,
cresc.
1
3

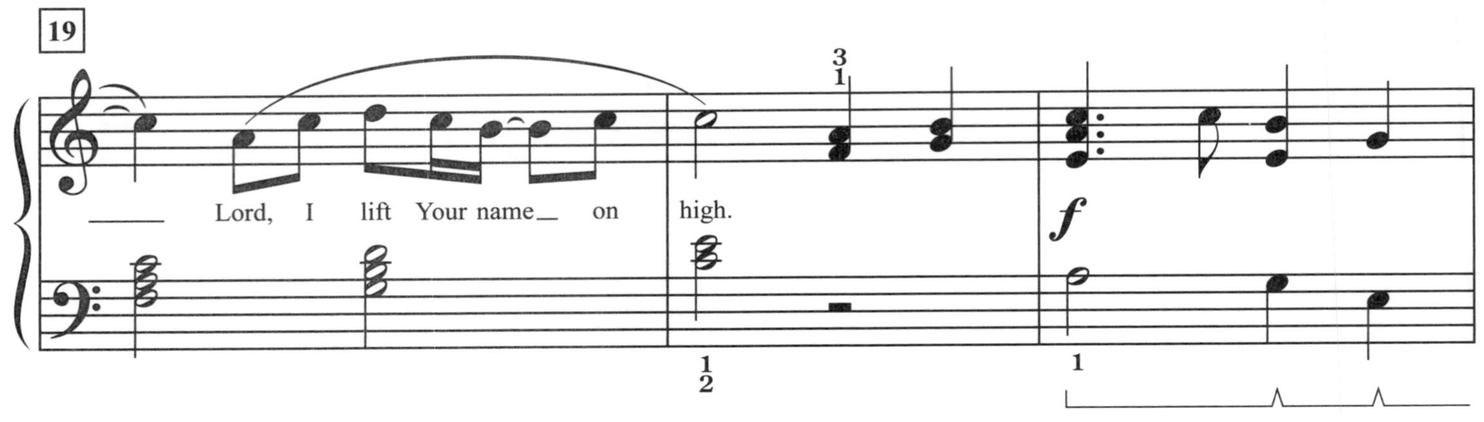
19
Lord, I lift Your name on high.
f

22
dim.
rit.

25
a tempo
mp
Lord, I lift Your name on high.
Lord, I love to sing Your

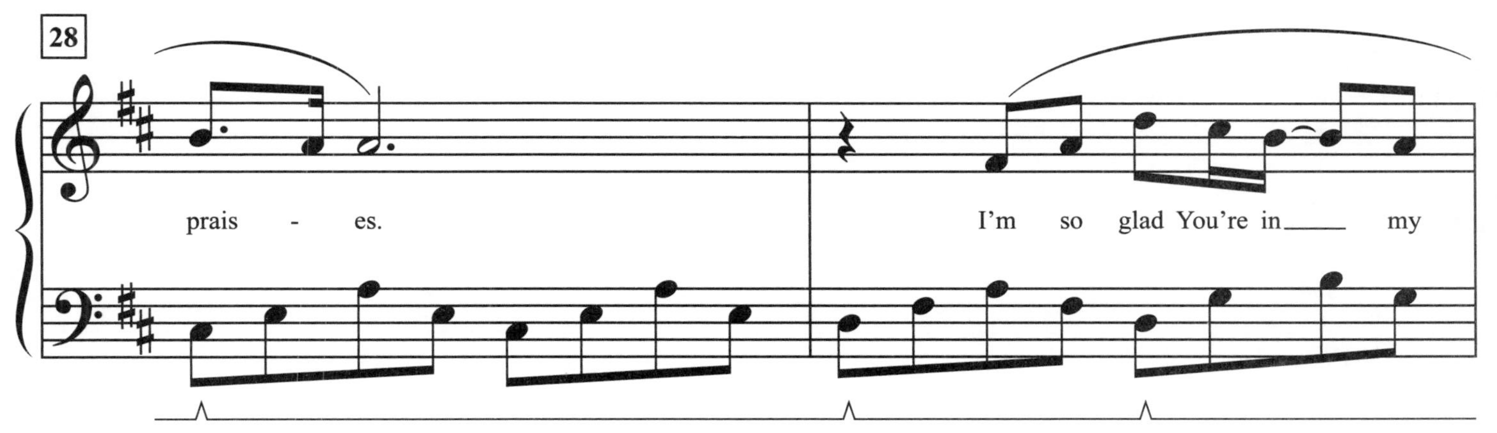
28
prais - es.
I'm so glad You're in my

30
life.
I'm so glad You came to

32
save us.
mf
You came from heav - en to earth

34
to show the way; from the earth to the cross, my debt to pay.
37
From the cross to the grave, from the grave to the sky,
39
Lord, I lift Your name on high.
Lord, I lift Your name on
42
high.
rit.
mp

We Fall Down

Words and Music by Chris Tomlin
Arranged by Carol Tornquist

10
mer - cy and love at the feet of Je - sus. And we cry,
13
"Ho - ly, ho - ly, ho - ly!" And we cry, "Ho - ly, ho - ly, ho -
16
- ly!" And we cry, "Ho - ly, ho - ly, ho - ly is the
19
Lamb!"

22
cresc.
poco rit.
And we cry,
a tempo
25
mf
"Ho - ly, ho - ly, ho - ly!" And we cry,
"Ho - ly, ho - ly, ho -
28
- ly!" And we cry,
"Ho - ly, ho - ly, ho - ly is the
Lamb!"
32
rit.

You Are My King (Amazing Love)

Words and Music by Billy Foote
Arranged by Carol Tornquist

Slowly, with expression

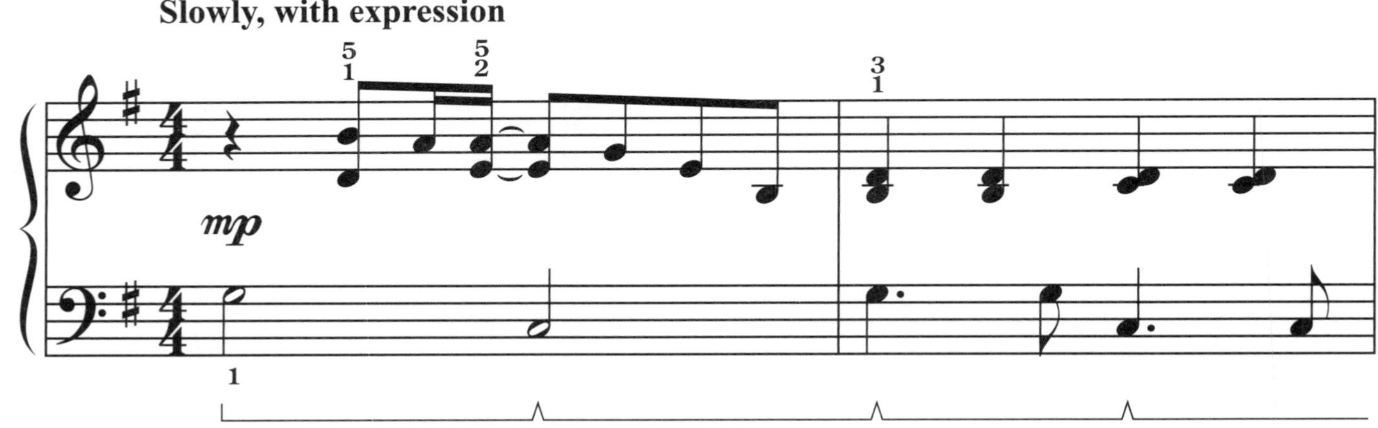

7
I'm ac - cept - ed;
You were con - demned.
9
I'm a - live and well, Your
Spir - it is with - in me be -
11
cause You died and rose a - gain.
13
mf
A - maz - ing love,
how can it be

15
that You, my King, would die for
me?
17
A - maz - ing love,
I know it's true;
19
1.
and it's my joy to hon - or
You.
21
2.
You. In all I
do I hon - or
You.

24
mp
You are my King! You are my
cresc. poco a poco
27
King! Je - sus, You are my King! Je - sus,
30
You are my King!
f
A - maz - ing love,
33
how can it be
that You, my King, would die for

35
me?
A - maz - ing love,
I know it's true;
38
1
2
and it's my joy to hon - or
You.
In all I
40
3
1
dim. poco a poco
do
I hon - or
4
You.
In all I
42
Very slowly
5
1
do
rit.
I hon - or
You.
mp
1
2

You're Worthy of My Praise

Words and Music by David Ruis
Arranged by Carol Tornquist

10
with all of my strength.
give You ev - 'ry - thing.
13
I will seek You all of my days.
I will lift up my eyes to Your throne.
16
I will fol - low
I will trust You, I will
19
all of Your ways.
trust You a - lone.
mf
I will give You

22
5
all my wor - ship,
I will give You
all my praise.
25
You a - lone I
long to wor - ship,
You a - lone are
28
1.
2.
5
wor - thy of my
praise.
mp
mp You a-lone are
5 2
32
Slowly
rit.
wor - thy of my
praise.
p